D. J. SMITH

Discovering
Horse-drawn Carriages

SHIRE PUBLICATIONS LTD

ACKNOWLEDGEMENTS

The author acknowledges with thanks the help received from the following: B. B. Murdock; K. Bennett; the Curator and staff of Birmingham Science Museum; the staff of Blakesley Hall Museum, Yardley, Birmingham; the Curator and staff of the Worcestershire County Museum.

The publishers acknowledge with thanks the assistance of Brian Wicks of Bath Carriage Museum.

Photographs are acknowledged as follows: City of Birmingham Museum and Art Gallery (photographs by Keith Bennett), plates 7, 9; Gunnersbury Park Museum (Copyright London Borough of Hounslow), plates 3, 20 and cover; The H.D.V. Series, plates 4, 14, 15, 23; Hull Transport Museum, plates 1, 5, 10, 11 (photograph by G. Bernard Wood), 16, 22, 26; Cadbury Lamb, plate 30; Raymond Lea, plates 2, 8, 18, 19, 24, 27; Leicester Transport Museum, plate 6; London Transport Executive, plate 13; Science Museum (Crown copyright), plate 12; Shuttleworth Collection (photograph by N. D. Welch), plate 28; B. Wicks, plates 17, 21; Burt Family Collection, plate 29; Studio Sark Photo, plate 31.

The cover photograph is of the Rothschild posting chariot at Gunnersbury Park Museum (see plate 3).

British Library Cataloguing in Publication data available.

Contents

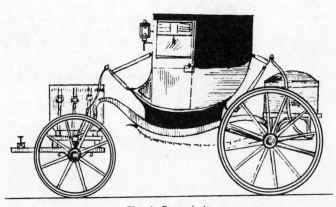

Fig. 1. Post-chaise.

Introduction

The term 'carriage' describes not only vehicles associated with ceremonial and social customs of a bygone era but a variety of types used for business and pleasure. While it may refer to the stately barouche and dress chariot at one end of the scale, it also includes the humble station bus, float and governess cart.

Before the advent of the motor-car, which was first known as a 'horseless carriage', there were equivalent types of horse-drawn vehicle to fulfil the needs of a large consumer market. Fords of Detroit were by no means the first business venture to use mass production for transport vehicles. Gigs, carts and buggies were turned out by the thousand from workshops geared to crude production-line methods, both in western Europe and North America. While master coach-builders provided more exclusive models for the upper classes, the small trader and commercial traveller relied on a plainer but no less serviceable vehicle, perhaps advertised on the front page of a local newspaper with details of cash-on-delivery and hire purchase.

Carriages varied not only in form and style but in size and type, there being both four-wheeled and two-wheeled vehicles. Further distinctions lay between privately owned owner-driven carriages and larger vehicles usually driven by coachmen. While the majority of carriages were privately owned there were also large numbers, including cabs and stage-coaches, termed 'public conveyances'.

While all coaches are also carriages, many open and semi-open carriages should not be termed coaches. A coach, at least from the end of the seventeenth century, was expected to have four wheels, a solid roof and springs. In modern terms the carriage is a vehicle drawn by a horse or pony, although there are notable exceptions such as hand-propelled and mechanically driven invalid carriages. At one time children drove small carriages drawn by goats or donkeys, while the infant King of Rome, later Napoleon II, was drawn in a carriage harnessed to a pair of sheep. In tropical countries such as India carriages have been drawn by asses, mules, oxen and even camels.

The word 'coach' derives from the Hungarian name for a small covered wagon, first used in Kotcze, its town of origin. Similar vehicles were later imported to Germany and France, known as *kutsche* or *coche* respectively.

1. The history of carriages

The earliest forms of vehicle for land transport were wooden sledges or slide-cars dragged either by humans or by animals. These were roughly made from branches, sometimes with a wickerwork basket for the load, which otherwise rested on cross-pieces or struts bound with leather thongs.

The first type of carriage with wheels developed from a slide-car of a kind used in parts of India and the Far East. A slide-car with added wheels was also recorded in Spanish cave paintings of the second millennium B.C. These would have been drawn by oxen using a neck yoke. Wheeled vehicles of various types were known to several early civilisations in Asia and Europe but for many centuries their development was hampered by the lack of good roads or even serviceable tracks. An exception may be found in the carts and primitive wagons used by nomadic tribesmen of central Asia and eastern Europe, able to roam over large areas of flat terrain with few mountains or forests to bar their progress.

The lighter forms of two-wheeled vehicle developed into chariots, used either in hunting or in warfare by the Assyrians, Ancient Egyptians, Babylonians and Persians. While the early types had solid or disc wheels, Egyptian wall paintings and Assyrian bas-reliefs show much lighter vehicles with elegantly spoked wheels. These were drawn by swift horses which closely resembled the Arab or barb of modern times. The number of wheel-spokes varied between eight and twelve on the Assyrian chariots to a mere four or six spokes on Egyptian vehicles. The rim of the wheel was also much deeper and more strongly constructed on vehicles of the Middle East, while those of Egypt — running over the flatter surface of the desert — were comparatively lighter.

Greek and Roman carriages

The Ancient Greeks had both two-wheeled and four-wheeled vehicles, but mainly the former on account of their mountainous, rock-strewn terrain. A four-wheeled ox wagon would be used for agriculture, while the two-wheeled chariot would be horse-drawn and mainly used for military purposes. Four-wheeled vehicles were occasionally used for transporting human passengers on pleasure excursions, but these were limited by poor roads, and in any case the Greeks regarded riding in carriages for pleasure as decadent and effeminate. People of all classes were expected to walk or ride horses, asses or mules. This did not prevent the use of war chariots for racing, which became a popular sport for young men as early as 776 B.C. The Greek chariot, later copied by Etruscans and Romans, had a high padded dashboard at the front and low-slung wheels. This design was intended to keep the centre of gravity low and prevent overturning at corners.

5

The first Roman vehicle of any importance was the *plaustrum* or dray, which was a platform on four wheels used mainly in agriculture. The first passenger vehicle was merely a chair fitted to the *plaustrum*, known as the *sella curulis*. This was used by governors travelling about the country to administer justice in remote areas. A further variety of *plaustrum*, used mainly in cities, was fitted with low superstructure and a canopy roof. This was originally limited to the official classes such as governors, senators, high-ranking priests and those officiating at public ceremonies. To own a carriage was considered a great personal honour granted only to the highest in the state.

While only the nobility and high-ranking officials used four-wheeled carriages, a lighter two-wheeled carriage or *carpentum* was used by lesser officials and the lower priesthood. This was also adapted as a bridal car in which the newly wedded bride was taken to the house of her husband. The *carpentum mortuarium* was a two-wheeled funeral carriage or hearse. The four-wheeled *pilentum* was a ceremonial carriage used by Vestal virgins and older women taking part in festive or funeral processions.

Civilians travelling over long distances, for business or pleasure, had the choice of two main types of vehicle. These were the *raeda* and the *carruca dormitoria*. The first was a lighter vehicle in which it was possible to rest on made-up couches. The second was a heavier or sleeping carriage with provision for special beds. The *essedum*, for shorter distances, was a two-wheeled vehicle, similar to a large chariot, of a type also known in Britain and Gaul.

During the Middle Ages the use of wheeled vehicles, except for agriculture, underwent a decline. Towns and cities were built on rivers and travel between them was often by means of barges or coastal shipping. As in ancient Greece, medieval folk who travelled overland went either on horseback or on foot. Only the aged and invalids made use of litters or wheeled vehicles, when these were available.

The first English carriages

The period of the Renaissance, from the end of the fifteenth century, was noted for a gradual return to higher living standards, at first limited to the nobility and wealthy merchants but later affecting other ranks and conditions of men. This eventually led to improved roads and better vehicles to travel over them. Yet it was not until the sixteenth century that wheeled vehicles became respectable for those who were fit enough either to walk or to ride on horseback.

Carriages and coaches were introduced into England during the second half of the sixteenth century. The first coach to be made in this country was constructed in 1555 by Walter Rippon for the Earl of Rutland. Henry Fitzallen, Earl of Arundel, imported a coach from Germany in 1580, and this was copied in large numbers for the use of the upper classes. Elizabeth I preferred her coaches to be designed and made by Dutch builders.

By the middle of the seventeenth century there were not only private coaches but also hackney coaches for public transport, while stage-coaches plied between the larger cities. Yet in England it was over a century before a serious attempt was made to improve the national system of trunk routes. Land travel was often a hazardous experience, beset not only by armed robbers but also by quagmire, ruts and potholes, in which a coach might sink or break its wheels and axles. The impossibility of overland journeys at certain seasons of the year led to the development of artificial waterways or canals for both goods and passengers. Roads with macadam surfaces, supported by the turnpike system of upkeep and repair, eventually revived inter-city road transport, although coaches were increasingly used in towns by the nobility throughout the second half of the seventeenth century.

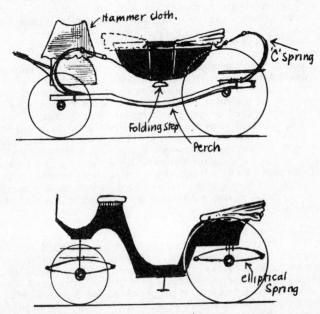

Fig. 2. (Above) Early carriage with underperch. (Below) Later type with elliptical springs, much lower, and with no perch and full lock.

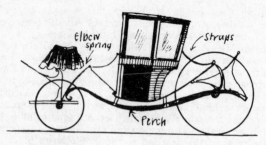

Fig. 3. Early coach with strap suspension.

Early developments

Early coaches were little more than boxes on wheels, heavy and cumbersome. Although a glass-sided coach was brought from Italy to France in 1620 there were very few vehicles with glass windows in western Europe before 1650. Up to that time empty window spaces, above the doors, were protected by leather curtains.

Steel springs were first introduced about 1670, before which bodywork was suspended on leather straps or braces from corner pillars of the rude undercarriage. Steel springs greatly reduced draught weight and enabled the vehicle to be lighter, smaller and more elegant. The first springs were uprights of laminated steel known as whip springs, later replaced by curved or elbow springs. Fifty years later elbow springs were replaced by C springs.

The eighteenth century was noted for perfecting the inventions of earlier periods rather than for producing innovations. 'Daleme' springing of the early eighteenth century was a combination of steel springs and strap suspension. This was named after a French clockmaker called Daleme, who is said to have invented coach springs. The C spring can also be traced back to the seventeenth century but was not widely used until the second half of the eighteenth century.

Wheels, tyres and axles

The correct type of wheel was an important feature of all road vehicles. About the middle of the seventeenth century 'dished' wheels began to make their appearance. 'Dishing' meant that wheels were cone-shaped, fixed to the ends of axles which were bent slightly downwards at each end of the axle-tree. When revolving, the lower spokes were always vertical. This made the 'dished' wheel stronger than other types and kept it more securely fixed to the axle. Large numbers of wheels were still made to the

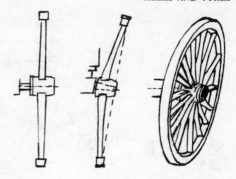

Fig. 4. (From left to right) Cross-section of straight wheel; cross-section of dished wheel; dished wheel.

original upright pattern, but these were mainly for lighter vehicles expected to travel over flatter surfaces.

Iron tyres were originally strakes or strips of metal fixed to the rims in sections. By 1767 a man named Hunt invented a metal band tyre which could be shrunk on to the wheel when red-hot. Solid rubber tyres and, later, pneumatic tyres were used during the second half of the nineteenth century, although frequently rejected — in the case of pneumatic tyres — as inelegant. Pneumatic tyres were first associated with a special type of four-wheeled cab that could be converted into an ambulance.

Axles or axle-trees, to which wheels were fixed, were not usually made by coach-builders but were the concern of specialists, both individuals and, later, large firms. The two main developments of hubs were known as the 'mail' or 'mail-coach' and the 'collinge'. The mail fitting secured the wheel by a system of three bolts passing through a plate into the nave or centre, while the collinge (of 1792) had cone-shaped naves held in place by external collets (collars) and centre nuts.

Draught gear, by which the horses drawing the coach or carriage were attached to the vehicle, was usually in the form of a centre pole and traces, with a horse harnessed to either side of the pole. The traces were attached to a horizontal splinter bar directly under the forecarriage, but sometimes to horizontal bars or swingletrees with a swingletree for each horse. If a team of four or more horses was used, the wheel horses, or those nearest the vehicle, were attached directly to the pole and splinter bar. Leaders were attached to swingletrees fitted to the head of the coach or carriage pole. Single-horse vehicles — with either two or four wheels — used shafts or parallel bars attached to either side of the horse. These latter were either curved or straight.

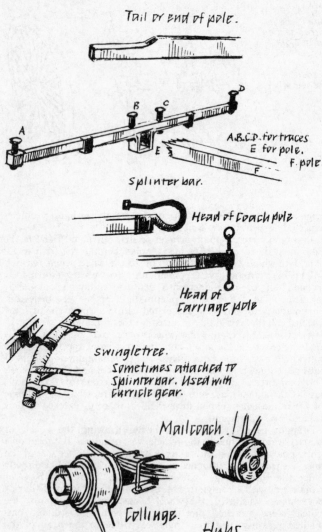

Tail or end of pole.

A.B.C.D. for traces
E for pole.
F. pole.

Splinter bar.

Head of Coach pole

Head of Carriage pole

Swingletree.
Sometimes attached to Splinter bar. Used with Curricle gear.

Mailcoach

Collinge.

Hubs.

Fig. 5. Draught gear, and (bottom) hubs.

The late eighteenth century

During the second half of the eighteenth century there was not only a great improvement in roads but also a considerable increase in the range and variety of carriages. It was towards the end of this era that the landau, barouche, post-chaise and gig were introduced, most of which survived in one form or another until the 1900s. By 1775 there were four hundred registered stage-coaches. The London to Manchester coach, running at least twice a week, made the journey in roughly 4½ days, although from 1815 times were recorded of less than eighteen hours. Coaches and carriages were taxed from 1747 while carriage horses were taxed from 1785.

From the mid eighteenth century many large and elaborate coaches were constructed for royalty and the wealthier nobles. In 1757 a state coach was built for the City of London which still appears in the Lord Mayor's Show. This was followed by the even more attractive State Coach of England in 1761, first used by George III. Many fine coaches were designed for the royal and

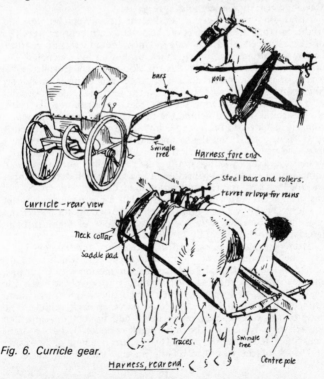

Fig. 6. Curricle gear.

imperial families of Europe, perhaps the finest being commissioned by the House of Hapsburg. Many of these are now on show in the Imperial Carriage Museum, Vienna. The state and coronation coaches used by Napoleon I are also admirable of their kind, although by the end of the eighteenth century styles were becoming more utilitarian.

Towards the end of the eighteenth century curricle harness was introduced for driving a pair of horses, usually with a special type of two-wheeled gig or curricle. This type of draught gear was based on a centre pole and cross-bar with rollers. The cross-bar was in effect T-shaped, its centre part fixed to the pole while cross-pieces were yoked to harness pads on the back of each horse. Other traces and links attached to the neck collar and pole at the fore end and to neck collar and swingletrees at the rear end. This form of draught harness was for swift, light work — noted for lack of noise and friction.

Developments in brakes and springs

Although several types of brake for heavy vehicles were introduced from the early part of the seventeenth century, very few of these proved of much value. Until the nineteenth century, hardly any attempt was made to use brakes on light vehicles. The most reliable form of check was the skid-pan, which was a metal wedge or plate attached to a rear wheel rendering it immobile. Skid-pans were adjusted, usually on the near side, at the summit of a steep hill to prevent a heavy coach overrunning its team. Rollers could be fitted behind the rear wheels to prevent a vehicle running backwards on a slope, but these were more frequently used on wagons. From the second half of the nineteenth century lever and pedal brakes were introduced. The making of hand-lever brakes was a highly skilled craft, great care being taken to prevent unnecessary rattle and vibration. It was considered that rubber was the best material for application to metal tyres while wood and cast iron acted better on rubber tyres. The long connecting bar of the lever brake was eventually replaced by a lighter and more convenient 'Bowden' wire, often passing out of sight through interior bodywork.

After prolonged use of C springs, the next development came with the introduction of elliptical leaf springs, which were invented in 1804. Although first used in conjunction with C springs, elliptical springs enabled coach-builders to dispense with the heavy bar or underperch which originally formed the main connection between front and back parts of each vehicle. The body of the vehicle, now much lower and lighter, developed to contain its own support, the underperch replaced by bars of light steel concealed under the body. The new arrangement allowed safe underlock of the forewheels while making the vehicle easier to drive. In this respect the original type of perch had limited the turning circle of the wheels.

The nineteenth century

A wide range of two-wheeled vehicles came into fashion shortly after the Napoleonic Wars (about 1817), followed by the four-wheeled park phaeton and pony phaeton of the 1820s. These latter were usually owner-driven, the pony phaeton being the particular favourite of George IV. The first half of the nineteenth century was the great age of driving, from the sporting viewpoint, although public coaches were soon to be eclipsed by the introduction of main-line railways. Wealthy amateurs and sprigs of the nobility had been driving both private and public coaches from the 1790s although the hobby increased in popularity until the second half of the nineteenth century. Even after the coming of railways, coaching was kept alive by private clubs such as the Four-in-Hand Club and the later Coaching Club.

Omnibuses were first used in the streets of Paris, but were brought to England, and greatly improved, in 1829. The Hansom cab, designed by a professional architect of that name (the designer of Birmingham Town Hall), was introduced in 1834 although greatly improved by other men a year or two later. The four-wheeled cab or 'growler', for many years the cheapest and most popular cab in London, came in about 1835, originally

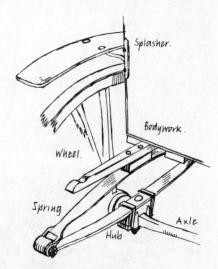

Fig. 7. Rear
suspension of a
pony phaeton.

13

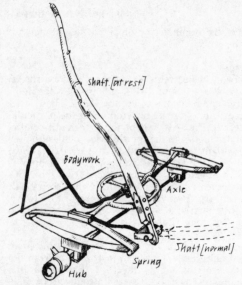

Fig. 8. Front
suspension of
a pony
phaeton.

having been driven as a family coach known as the clarence.
Earlier hackney coaches were usually the discarded town coaches
of the nobility, drawn by two horses.

Perhaps the most popular of the smaller coach-driven vehicles
was the brougham, designed for and named after Lord Brougham,
a celebrated Whig statesman of the period. This was introduced in
1838/9 although a greatly improved version came in 1845. The
brougham was the last original type of four-wheeled carriage,
surviving until the age of mechanical road transport.

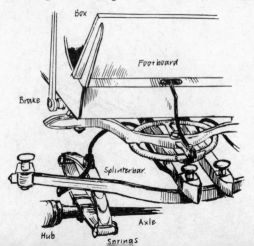

Fig. 9. Fore-
carriage and
undergear of
four-wheeled
vehicle,
suitable for
two or four
horses.

2. Builders, materials and finish

The craft of building coaches and carriages eventually employed many craftsmen and highly skilled workers, ranging from heraldic painters to bodymakers or builders, wheelwrights and lamp-makers. Although formerly most of the parts were made under the same roof, there was a growing tendency by the middle of the eighteenth century towards specialisation. This led to subcontracts for many fittings, including axle-trees and springs.

Some builders specialised in certain types of vehicle and were unable or unwilling to produce anything very different from that to which they were accustomed. Sharp and Bland of South Audley Street specialised in larger, heavier vehicles and were unable to satisfy Lord Brougham when he commissioned them to construct a small, neat carriage for town work. The order was later transferred to Robinson and Cook of Mount Street with satisfactory results.

Basic materials
Just as a number of different skills was represented in the making of coaches and carriages, a quantity of different materials was also used. The chief of these were wood and metal, used for bodywork and the chassis or undercarriage.

Ash and oak were the most valued timber; ash being coppice grown. Ash was used mainly for the framework of the body, being a tough fibrous wood lacking elasticity and unlikely to warp or twist. Oak, usually of young growth, was used for underframes and wheel-spokes. Elm was ideal for planks, wheel-naves and hubs but, having a wavy or strongly marked grain, was difficult to paint. Mahogany was used for interior and exterior panels, being favoured for its smooth surface and the ease with which it could be either painted or polished. If panels were to be covered with leather or fabric, however, a cheaper type of cedar was used in place of mahogany.

Iron was the chief metal, being used for bars, hoops, hinges, stays, axles, bolts, nails, tyres and plates. Steel was mainly used for springs and suspension bars. Copper was for beading and sheathing. Brass was for buckles, rings, plates and wheel-hoops. Superior axle-tree nuts were made from gunmetal. All other metals and alloys were used for decorative work and small accessories.

Upholstery and paintwork
Interior trim related to well fitted seats, of maximum comfort, upholstered according to individual taste or fashions of the day.

Leather, was one of the traditional forms of upholstery but by the middle of the eighteenth century there was a preference for figured tabaret and a variety of hard-wearing satins. Tabaret is a silk stuff with alternating stripes of satin surface and watered surface, much favoured by coach trimmers and furnishers. From the late 1870s there was a revival of leather coverings and the finest quality upholstery was produced in morocco leather. Side curtains were made of silk lutestring, a stiff satin-surfaced material. The floors would be covered with either Brussels carpeting or fitted velvet-pile rugs.

Paintwork for exterior finish was an important aspect of coach-building, affecting not only appearance but durability. Many coats of paint, alternating between white lead and yellow ochre, were first laid on as swiftly as possible. When these had thoroughly hardened, after two or three weeks, all paintwork was rubbed down with pumice-stone and water, until grain and brush marks were hidden and the surface made thoroughly smooth. Two further coats of white lead were then applied and rubbed down with sandpaper. The main colours of green or brown, etc, were then applied over the sanded surface, up to three coats. Afterwards frames and underparts were blackened and allowed to dry, before the application of six coats of copal varnish. Two qualities of varnish were used, the best and hardest being reserved for wheels and underparts. As a final touch before polishing, all unplated metal parts were japanned. At least eighteen to twenty coats of paint were used for a first-class job. After the vehicle had been used for several months the brilliant gloss, especially on the body panels, could be revived and improved by further hand polishing. This would be done by a specialist using oil and rottenstone. Rottenstone was a decomposed silicious form of limestone deprived of its calcareous or chalky matter, widely used as a polishing agent for metal and paintwork.

Lamps were usually round on dress coaches and carriages and square on travelling carriages. Most were lit by candles but later oil and even battery lamps were used. The best wax candles were preferred, contained in tinplate tubes, being forced gradually upwards by coiled springs as they burned down. Candle lamps were always reliable and much cleaner than oil lamps.

3. National designs and their origins

The English coach was traditionally flat-roofed with straighter sides than Continental models. French coaches were renowned for having convex roofs and curving side walls, while those of Germany and the countries of central and eastern Europe had sides that were even more strongly curved.

While the heavier types of four-wheeled coaches were associated with long-distance travel in northern or eastern Europe, lighter two-wheeled vehicles descended from the *carretta* or pony-cart of Mediterranean countries, especially Italy and Sicily (plate 1). This was mainly because two-wheeled vehicles were better for the mountainous conditions of southern Europe. In thinly populated areas of eastern Europe, where towns and settlements were long distances apart, covered carriages such as the britschka were greatly favoured, as these could be converted into sleeping compartments.

American designs

American designers followed French rather than English traditions in coach and carriage building. This was mainly because French vehicles were lighter but stronger than those of other nations, better suited to the badly made roads of a colonial country. According to European tastes, however, many American vehicles seemed to lack form and elegance. American designs greatly improved — from an aesthetic viewpoint — towards the end of the nineteenth century, but for many years wealthy Americans imported their carriages either from London or Paris.

The most typical American vehicle was the buggy, not to be confused with more elegant European versions of the same vehicle or a two-wheeled carriage of the same name but different appearance and purpose. The American buggy developed from a tray-bodied (*i.e.* with a broad platform and low sides) German vehicle of the early nineteenth century, usually hooded. Such vehicles were used for both town and country driving from the early 1820s until the First World War. A few, however, survived in remote areas until the late 1930s. Elliptical springs were mounted in a crosswise position, a form of suspension imitated by the first T model Ford, which may be described as a mechanical buggy. American buggies were equirotal (front wheels being the same size as back wheels) or near equirotal. There were several different versions used in all parts of North America but seldom seen in other parts of the world.

4. Methods of driving

A vehicle with passenger seats, having four wheels, was usually driven from a raised seat or box-seat above the forecarriage. In the case of the dress chariot and the state coach this was covered with an elaborate drapery known as a hammercloth, protected by a waterproof sheet in wet weather. Many smaller vehicles had a combined front seat for two, usually with a back-rest, the driver sitting on the right-hand side. With the float and the governess cart, driver and passengers entered through a rear door, sitting on either lengthwise or crosswise seats well back in the body of the vehicle. In the governess cart the driver could sit on either side of the vehicle, but half turned in his seat. Allowance was made for this by having a seat on each side partly cut away to make room for the driver's legs.

Postilions

Fast carriages on good roads, especially the travelling chariot and the post-chaise, were driven by outriders or postilions who rode on the near-side horse of a pair and led its partner. Although vehicles of the latter type were seen on the roads of England from the mid eighteenth until the early nineteenth century, they were more in evidence on the better roads of Europe, especially before British roads were improved by Telford and McAdam. In England the post-chaise in particular was an expensive alternative to the stage-coach. For many years there was an undeclared war between postboys and the drivers of stage-coaches; it was a contest the stage-coach drivers won, for stage-coaches remained in service some years after post-chaises disappeared. Postboys, or postilions in the public service, could be hired with their teams at certain inns known as posting houses, these being at intervals of eight or ten miles apart. Driving from the box, however, was an established British tradition and very few of the family or state coaches of the upper classes were postilion-driven.

The reason why traffic in Britain drives on the left is because most people are right-handed and the coachman in charge of a British team would tend to sit on the right-hand side of the box. The postilion or postboy rode on the near or left-hand horse, using his whip on the right-hand horse. It was also a natural preference to keep the ridden horse nearer the crown of the road than the gutter; when postilions were outnumbered by coachmen they had to follow the rules and tastes of the majority. The thirteen American colonies also kept their traffic on the left of the road but changed to the right or Continental drive during the War of Independence, perhaps out of deference to their French allies.

Methods of harnessing teams

Driven horses were usually harnessed as singles (one horse), pairs (two horses abreast), tandem (two horses, one behind the other), threes (three horses abreast), unicorn (two horses behind and one in front), four-in-hand (one pair in front and one pair behind) and sixes (three pairs behind each other). There were no upper limits to the number that could be driven although a team of more than four horses was rarely seen after the second half of the eighteenth century, except on occasions of state ceremonial or for trick driving. With six or more horses on the road the leading pair was usually managed by a postilion. A coach or carriage on a steep hill might be assisted by an extra horse at the front, known as a 'cock horse', ridden by a youth or small boy. Boys on cock horses were often stationed near steep hills, in towns and cities, to assist heavier vehicles. In the main streets of Paris, which from the early nineteenth century were much wider than those of London, buses were frequently drawn by three or more horses abreast. The Russians frequently drove a light carriage to a team of three abreast, known as a troika, although only the centre horse was in draught (at the trot) while the outside horses cantered with arched necks merely for show.

From the end of the eighteenth century a number of daring young men, usually bucks of the Regency period, drove high-seated gigs or cocking carts with a pair of horses or ponies in tandem. This was highly dangerous, especially where there were many turnings and crossings, and almost suicidal in heavy traffic. Although such daring was less popular during the staid Victorian era, there were always a few who preferred to drive in this manner, which experienced a revival at the turn of the century. Even today there may be the chance of seeing a gig driven tandem at a horse show, in one of the light harness classes. Driving in this way was known as 'tooling a tandem'.

Fig. 10. Berline, later version.

5. Coachman-driven carriages

Carriages driven by coachmen were four-wheeled vehicles usually heavier than privately driven or owner-driven carriages. With a few exceptions they were driven to either a pair or four-in-hand. The main distinctions lay between travelling carriages for long-distance work and town carriages, subdivided between those for either formal or informal occasions.

The berline

A coach said to have been invented by a famous designer of the seventeenth century named Roubo, the berline was a four-seater vehicle almost equally popular in France and Germany, used for both long-distance work and semi-formal occasions. An improved version of the mid eighteenth century was first built in Berlin — then capital of Prussia — after which city it was named. The strapping or braces of the second version partly supported the underside of the bodywork and restrained lateral sway, a great disadvantage of C springs. There were two underperches on either side of the vehicle, high enough to allow underlock of the forewheels. This made the driver's seat or box very high above ground level. There was usually a rear platform for two or more standing footmen, who held on to the roof by means of looped leather straps. The berline was drawn by either two or four horses.

The halbberline

A coupé or cut-down version of the berline, mainly popular during the 1780s, the halbberline seated two inside passengers. Bodywork was similar to that of the travelling chariot and post-chaise. The forewheels were much smaller than those of the berline, while the box-seat was correspondingly lower.

The landau

In its original form the landau was imported from Germany during the closing decades of the eighteenth century. It was a semi-closed carriage with a double hood and could be used in all weather conditions. On early vehicles the hoods were made of harness leather and fell back a mere forty-five degrees. In wet weather the interior could be uncomfortably hot and stuffy. To keep the leather smart and flexible, exteriors were treated with oil and blacking which in no way improved its odour. Bodywork of earlier types was square and awkward with the floor dropped to a much lower level than the seats. It was thus uncharacteristic of average Continental designs in general and German designs in particular. Later, more elegant types had deeper, curved bodies and were known as **canoe-landaus** (plate 2). During the second

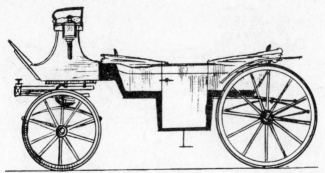

Fig. 11. Landau.

half of the nineteenth century great improvements were made to the hoods, which eventually folded almost flat. Landaus were drawn by either two or four horses.

Landaus held four passengers with room on the box for coachman and groom. Some versions in royal service also had rear seating for two carriage footmen.

There were two smaller versions, both seating two passengers, known as **landaulets.** The first type, introduced during the 1790s, had a box-seat for two. The landaulet of the mid nineteenth century, sometimes known as a **fly,** was drawn by a single horse and widely used in country districts as a station cab.

Like many open and semi-open carriages the under-body of the landau was often reinforced with a steel plate. This function — holding the vehicle together — was performed in a coach by the roof and sides.

The calèche

This was a type of carriage widely used in all parts of Europe from the late eighteenth century, similar in many respects to the canoe-landau. In Germany it was known as the *Kalesche* and in England as the calash. Although usually drawn by four horses it was slightly smaller and lighter than the landau. A later version, sometimes adapted as a travelling carriage, had a complex form of suspension and was known as the **eight-spring calèche.** There were both elliptical and C springs supporting rear carriage and forecarriage, with an underperch and straps or braces to prevent sway. It could seat four persons with room for the coachman and footman on the box.

The barouche

Another vehicle of the late eighteenth century, the barouche originated in France but was also popular in Britain and Germany

Fig. 12. Barouche.

by the turn of the century. It could be drawn by two or four horses, although six were sometimes used on formal or dress occasions. It appeared either with or without a box, its team sometimes in the charge of postilions. A semi-open carriage, its hood could be raised from the rear half only. Two passengers normally faced a windscreen directly behind the box, when the hood was raised. There was frequently a rear seat or rumble for two or more attendants.

The travelling chariot

A type of privately owned post-chaise used by the nobility and high-ranking officers, the travelling chariot (plate 3) was very often used for touring in Continental countries. The doors were usually decorated with a family crest or monogram, while a notable feature would be a sword-case at the rear of the vehicle, containing either dress or uniform swords. The travelling chariot, unlike the post-chaise, often had a rumble seat for grooms and family servants. Two or four horses were used, under the control of postilions or postboys. While privately owned horses may have been used for the first and last stages of a long journey, intermediate stages depended on horses and drivers from post-houses along the route.

Travelling chariots were mainly popular between 1795 and 1825. Vehicles of this type, discarded by their wealthy owners, were often bought cheaply and converted into post-chaises.

The britschka

A large and often cumbersome vehicle, the britschka was introduced from Hungary, via Austria and Germany, about 1818. A flat-bottomed structure, it could be converted into a sleeping carriage by raising the sides and hood. Widely used on the Continent for long-distance travel, it was also favoured by royal

Fig. 13. Britschka.

messengers and embassy staff, frequently carrying the diplomatic bag. The engineer Isambard Kingdom Brunel lived in a britschka for several weeks on end, while surveying the main line of the Great Western Railway. It was driven from the box or by postilions, usually to a team of four or six.

A smaller version introduced from France, about 1821, was known as the **dormeuse.** This frequently had a hooded and partly enclosed rumble seat for servants.

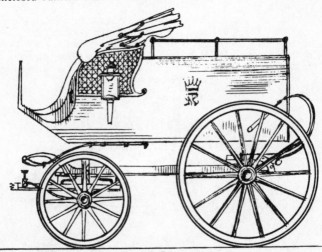

Fig. 14. Fourgon.

The fourgon

A large four-wheeled composite carriage, the fourgon was partly used for luggage, but had an enlarged box-seat for personal servants such as maids, valets and footmen. It was sent ahead of a travelling carriage or chariot and, when touring abroad, was in the care of a special courier, escorted by armed guards. The idea was to arrive some time ahead of the main party and assist with the preparation of rooms and unpacking of luggage. The modern fourgon is a luggage van at the head of a Continental passenger train.

The droshky

A light, open carriage of Russian origin, the droshky was fashionable in several parts of Europe after the Napoleonic Wars, especially during the early 1820s. Built with both a light underperch and C springs, it was fairly low-slung, its rear seat being less than twelve inches above the hind axle-tree. The original version carried four passengers, two facing each other, and was driven from the box. Later versions were smaller and carried only two passengers. In England the droshky was drawn either by one or two horses, according to size and weight. In Russia a **troika** — three horses abreast — was more frequently used. A later English version, adapted for town driving, was known as the **pilentum.** This latter was designed and manufactured by David Davies of Albany Street, London.

The vis-à-vis

A narrow form of closed carriage used on ceremonial or dress occasions, the vis-à-vis usually carried two people facing one another. First introduced in France about 1768 and reintroduced in England about 1820, it was not widely used after the reign of George IV. The name is wrongly used for other carriages and coaches in which the passengers sit opposite each other.

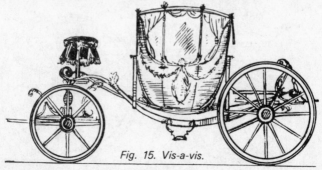

Fig. 15. Vis-a-vis.

The sociable

A semi-open vehicle of the 1860s and 1870s driven from the box to a pair of horses, the sociable seated four passengers and was a cross between a barouche and a victoria. It was often known as a barouche-sociable.

The dress chariot

The dress chariot, a nobleman's closed carriage (plate 5), used on ceremonial or dress occasions, was introduced during the 1830s. It was similar to the earlier travelling chariot but was usually driven from the box to a pair of horses. The box-seat was covered with an elaborate mantle or hammercloth, trimmed with deep fringes. Door panels were painted with a crest or monogram. Footmen in full dress livery — usually wearing feather-trimmed cocked hats — stood on a rear platform between the C springs. At least two of them would carry long staves with which to defend the coach in a riot or clear the way through crowded streets. The forward-looking cross-seat of the interior was designed for two passengers facing a glass panel behind the box.

Favourite horses would be Cleveland bays or Yorkshire coach-horses of matching bay colour.

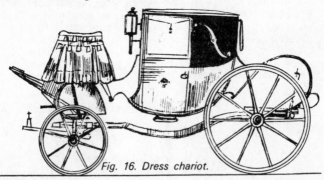

Fig. 16. Dress chariot.

The state coach

A larger and slightly more up-to-date version of the dress chariot, the state coach was used on formal occasions. Seating four people face to face, it had three glass windows on either side and was frequently known as a **glass coach.** Popular during the late 1840s it is still used for state ceremonial. It was drawn either by a pair or four-in-hand, but sometimes by a team of six. Like the dress chariot the box displayed an ornate hammercloth. Harness was also ornate and the manes and tails of the matching coach-horses would be plaited with strands of coloured braid.

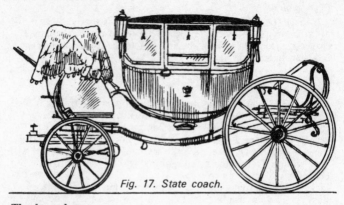

Fig. 17. State coach.

The brougham

A small carriage of the late 1830s, originally designed to carry two inside passengers facing forwards, the brougham was driven from the box to a single horse. It was named after the first Lord Brougham for whom it was built, to his ideas if not to his personal designs (plate 4). The first version, by Sharp and Bland, was too heavy and far from being a success. Later versions were greatly improved by Robinson and Cook. The basic idea was for something light and handy, mainly for informal occasions, on the same lines as a cab but with improved comfort and visibility. A much later version of the 1880s was known as the **bow-fronted brougham,** having a curved glass windscreen directly behind the box.

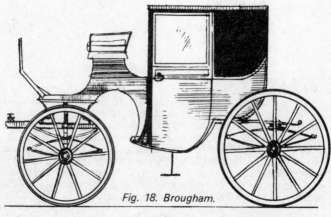

Fig. 18. Brougham.

The clarence

A modest family conveyance usually drawn by a single horse and driven from the box, the clarence (plate 6) was slightly larger than the brougham. It could seat four passengers and sometimes had a luggage rack on the roof. It was introduced in 1842 by the firm of Laurie and Marner of Oxford Street. Discarded clarences were often used as four-wheeled cabs and later designed as such, with slight modifications. A more fanciful and ornate version, also introduced by Laurie and Marner, was known as the **sovereign.**

The victoria

The victoria (illustrated on the cover) has long been considered one of the most elegant of all coachman-driven vehicles. It evolved about 1860, some claiming its descent from the pony phaeton. First used in Paris, it was greatly admired by the Prince of Wales, later Edward VII, and was also favoured by Queen Victoria, after whom an English version was named. Fashionable on account of royal patronage, it remained popular until the 1900s, especially as a parade or display carriage. Driven from the box to either a single horse or a pair, it carried two passengers facing forwards. A later, much larger version, to seat four passengers, was known as the double victoria. There were no doors to either version, which enabled the ladies of the period to make a becoming display of their flowing skirts.

A similar but far less elegant carriage had been used both in England and on the Continent, during the 1830s; it was known as a **milord.** The **panel-boot victoria** had a single folding seat behind the box-seat.

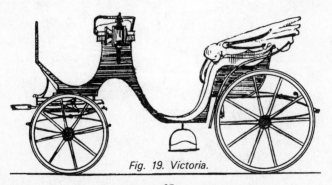

Fig. 19. Victoria.

The private omnibus or station bus

A general utility vehicle for both passengers and luggage, the private omnibus was widely used at weekend and country-house parties, for conveying personal servants and luggage to and from the station. First used about 1870, it was popular until the 1900s. Mainly in private hands, some were owned by hotels, while others were owned or hired by railway companies and used where a station was some distance from the nearest village.

It was usually driven from a box, high above the front of the vehicle, to either a pair or four-in-hand. Smaller versions were driven to a single horse. An example of the one-horse version, now exhibited at York Railway Museum, belonged to the Kent and Sussex Railway Company and was based on Tenterden station.

The larger versions carried between six and eight passengers, seated both inside and outside. Smaller types carried four or six only (inside) with luggage on the roof. Those in private ownership had interior linings of quilted satin with blinds over the windows. Entered by means of a back door and step, seating was longitudinal inside and latitudinal or crosswise on top.

Fig. 20. Private omnibus.

6. Public conveyances

The brouette
A French invention of 1668, the brouette was a form of sedan chair for one passenger only, which could be drawn by a man between the shafts in the style of an oriental rickshaw. A later version, known in England as the **sedan cart,** seated either one or two passengers and was drawn by a single horse, the driver running alongside.

The mail-coach
Perhaps the best known and certainly the most romantic of all public vehicles was the mail-coach. It was designed by John Palmer of Bath in 1784 and was a four-wheeled coach adapted to carry His Majesty's mails. The first service ran between London and Bristol, but by 1807 had extended as far west as Penzance, as far east as Yarmouth and as far north as Berwick-on-Tweed. In Wales the mail-coach reached Holyhead in the north and Milford Haven in the south, with routes through central Wales to Aberystwyth and Newtown. Key centres such as York, Shrewsbury, Exeter, Oxford, Brecon, Canterbury and Birmingham were at the junction of several routes, all services radiating from London.

Mail-coaches were hired to the Government and constructed by a firm of coach-builders known as John Vidler and Company of Millbank, London. They were painted in the royal livery of scarlet, maroon and black with the royal arms on the door panels. The guard-in-charge wore a scarlet livery and sat with the mailbags in a special locker under his feet. He was armed to defend the coach with a blunderbuss and pistols, while he also carried a long-stemmed horn for sounding warnings. The regulation horn was three feet in length and known to the coaching fraternity as a 'yard of tin'. Many guards provided their own horn of silver, copper or brass. Guards of mail-coaches, however, were not allowed to play tunes on the key bugle, favoured by guards on stage-coaches.

The first 'Palmer' coach was similar in outward appearance to a later version of the berline. It was slung fairly high on elbow springs at the front and C springs at the back. Box-seat and bodywork were mounted on a heavy perch. There were no outside seats for passengers and the guard shared a box with the driver. The luggage of the four inside passengers was stowed either on the roof or between the C springs.

A later version dating from the 1800s had outside seats for four passengers, with the guard seated at the rear. The perch was equally strong but lighter in appearance while the bodywork was balanced on side and transverse semi-elliptical springs, at both

Fig. 21. Mail-coach (1837).

front and back. The passenger compartment was mounted in the midst of a box-shaped structure, prominent at either end. The rear seat for the guard was mounted on curved irons with back and arm rests. An upholstered seat for three would be part of the roof, directly in front of the luggage space. This would have a back-rest, arm-rests on either side, and padded cushions. A box-seat for two would be mounted directly in front of the transverse seat for three, although having a padded back-rest for the passenger only. A three-aspect lamp was often fitted to the centre front of the driver's footboard. There would be two headlamps and two slightly smaller side lamps, placed in front of the coach doors on either side of the passenger compartment.

Suspension of the later mail-coach and stage-coach was by means of 'Telegraph' springs, first used on a stage-coach of that name. These comprised four semi-elliptical springs at both back and front of the underbody. There was a set of two longitudinal and two transverse springs, united by D links. This arrangement was similar to the eight-spring calèche.

The four-horse teams, also hired for the purpose, were driven on stages of from seven to ten miles, according to local gradients and the state of the roads. Average speed for the fastest coaches was 10¼ miles per hour. The only named mail-coach, running between London and Falmouth, was known as *Quicksilver*. It covered the 176 miles from London to Exeter in sixteen hours, allowing for changes of horses and halts for meals or Post Office business. Timekeeping was so accurate that people living along the route of mail-coaches would set their clocks by them.

The stage-coach

The first stage-coaches ran between some of the larger towns and cities of Britain during the second half of the seventeenth century, being larger versions of the town coaches of the nobility. It was not until the second half of the eighteenth century that they began to resemble the stage-coaches of Christmas card and legend. Many eventually ran in competition with the first mail-coaches, but during the eighteenth century were cheaper, less fashionable and not so well protected from highway robbers. They became more popular during the early nineteenth century, when driving was a craze, and it was possible to drive the coach if the official driver was either friendly or open to bribery.

In many respects later versions of the stage-coach bore a superficial resemblance to the mail-coach but carried more passengers. Later vehicles (plate 8) would take fourteen on top, not including driver and guard. Unlike the sober mail-coach in its royal livery, stage-coaches were painted in gaudy colours and had their names, also destinations, painted on side and back panels (plates 7 and 9). Some even displayed paintings of horseshoes, running foxes, crossed whips or the grinning mask of a fox. Typical names would be *Tally Ho, Red Rover* or *Experiment*. Night coaches plied during the hours of darkness, and were often cheaper, slower but less reliable. They were horsed by creatures of poor conformation, some actually blind, not respectable enough for daytime duties. These would be the proverbial 'three blind 'uns and a bolter'.

Conditions for driving coaches greatly improved with the introduction of macadamised road surfaces. The stage-coach driver became the hero of all right-minded schoolboys, while wealthy amateurs frequently drove their own coaches or worked for leading coach firms such as Chaplin and Horne. A stop to change horses would draw crowds to a village street, as if by magic. Large numbers thronged the yards of London coaching inns such as the Peacock at Islington, merely to applaud their favourite driver or admire outgoing teams. The first stage out of London was usually horsed by the best teams in the stud, with both coaches and horses decorated in honour of Christmas, the first of May or a great victory such as Trafalgar.

Short stage-coaches, slightly smaller than the inter-city or four-in-hand versions, ran between smaller towns or suburbs, up to twenty miles in distance. These were usually two-horse coaches eventually replaced by omnibuses.

The stage-wagon

Sometimes spelt 'waggon', this may be termed the poor man's stage-coach. Like the stage-coach it plied between larger centres in all parts of the country, but carried an even larger proportion of luggage and merchandise. The average stage-wagon, operating from about 1700, was a large panel-sided vehicle, the wheels having broad treads which not only helped to bear the load but flattened out ruts and potholes for other traffic. The wagon services operated in spring and summer only, being totally unsuitable for conditions of ice, snow and deep mire. They were drawn by teams of heavy horses — either ten or twelve in number — urged forward by drivers walking alongside with heavy cart whips. Later, drivers learned to control their teams from the back of a small but agile pony. Passengers were protected from the worst of wind and rain by a cover of heavy canvas, stretched over tilts or hoops, although the ends might have been open.

The normal pace was little better than a crawl, while the motion was rough and jolting so that many people preferred to walk beside the wagon for at least part of the journey. Even the stage-coach was forced to unload its passengers on steep hills, especially before the improvements of Telford and McAdam. In times of accident or difficulty passengers might be expected to help drag the vehicle out of a ditch or mudhole.

The touring coach

This was a vehicle very similar to the later type of stage-coach, sometimes a converted road coach in regular service. Later examples were purpose-built, being smaller but less elegant than the road coach. The touring coach was of compact, solid construction with forewheels small enough to turn in full lock. Seats on the roof were much higher than those of a stage-coach or private drag, all facing forward. Outside passengers were thus higher than the driver. The proportions of both front and back wheels resembled those of a cart or wagon rather than those of a coach.

Coaching tours, lasting from a few hours to a whole day, were especially popular during the 1890s and 1900s, but continued in some areas until the 1930s. The main centres were picturesque parts of Scotland, Wales, the Lake District and West of England. Both Llandudno and Colwyn Bay were great coaching centres running regular trips of up to fifty-six miles through the mountains of Snowdonia in about seven and a half hours with an hour for lunch at the Waterloo Hotel, Betws-y-Coed. Some of the later Llandudno coaches were so popular that they were converted from fourteen to twenty-two seaters, excluding coachman and guard. Some coaches were known as 'dummies', appearing to have an inside passenger compartment but with a roof too low for internal use.

The coffin cab

Similar in some respects to the later Hansom cab, the coffin cab was driven by a 'cabbie' either perched at the side or running in

1. A carretta (c. 1925), of a type in regular use almost unchanged from the Middle Ages to the 1950s in Italy and Sicily, and ancestor of many kinds of two-wheeled vehicle.

2. A one-horse landau of the canoe type (c. 1899), seen in Windsor.

3. A posting chariot, probably built in Austria at the end of the eighteenth century, and used by Nathan Mayer Rothschild. Now at Gunnersbury Park Museum, London.

4. The original brougham, built in 1838; this photograph was taken in 1939.

5. A town or dress chariot (c. 1860), bearing the arms of
the Earl of Yarborough of Brocklesby Park. It was used mainly
in London as a court carriage.

6. A clarence at a museum in Leicester.

7. The 'Old Times' stage-coach, which ran between Chester and Shrewsbury during the early nineteenth century, now at Blakesley Hall, Birmingham.

8. A stage-coach in action at the South Bucks Show, Hartwell.

9. *Under-gear of the 'Old Times' coach, showing splinter bar and attachment for the pole. Note the Telegraph springs.*

10. *Two-wheeled Hansom cab of the bow-fronted type (c. 1889). This particular cab was in use in Hull till the early 1920s.*

11. *A three-wheeled Hansom cab.*

12. *A model of George Shillibeer's three-horse omnibus of 1829.*

13. A garden-seat omnibus photographed in service in London about 1905.

14. A continental chaise; this finely carved model was photographed at the Royal Agricultural Society's Centenary Show in 1939.

15. This curricle, fitted with pneumatic tyres, was photographed in use c. 1900.

16. A cabriolet of around 1820, bearing the arms of the Goldsmid family.

17. *A tandem cart from Bath Carriage Museum.*

18. *A Stanhope gig.*

19. A Liverpool gig.

20. A pony phaeton of the late nineteenth century, used by an Isleworth firm to collect rents. Now in Gunnersbury Park Museum, London.

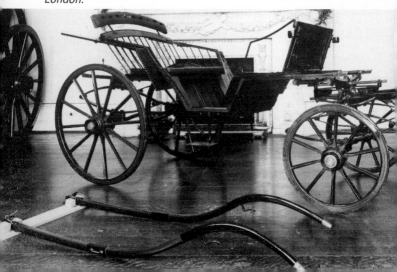

21. *A demi-mail phaeton exhibited in Bath Carriage Museum.*

22. Dogcart, c. 1860, a popular country and sporting carriage.

23. Pony-sized ralli car, built by Windovers of London. This vehicle, owned by J. Smith, Esq. of Ashingdon, Essex, has been called the finest in England.

24. Floats were general utility vehicles for the countryman, later adapted for urban milk delivery. The left-hand vehicle is a modern version.

25. A governess cart, c. 1900, driven by a donkey.

26. *This two-horse body brake of 1895 was in use until the 1920s.*

27. *A park drag in action at Windsor Horse Show.*

28. *Side view of an American buggy.*

29. *A vis-a-vis phaeton owned and driven by Mr Burt of Pattishall, Northamptonshire.*

30. A governess cart.

31. A wagonette photographed in 1968 in Sark, Channel Islands, where motor vehicles are banned.

the road. Wheels were much smaller than those of the hansom while the name derived from the resemblance of the roof of the vehicle to an up-ended coffin. Popular during the second half of the eighteenth century, it seated a single passenger.

A later version of the coffin cab, known as the London cab, was introduced about 1823. This had slightly larger wheels and a hood that could be raised or lowered according to the weather. It was driven from a side-seat over the off-side wheel, and seated two passengers.

The American cab

A two-wheeled cab of the 1830s, drawn by a single horse, the American cab was introduced in the streets of New York but later copied, for a brief period, in London. It seated four passengers on longitudinal seats, two on each side, and was entered through a rear door by means of a low step. The driver sat on the roof at the front.

The Hansom cab

The original hansom was a square and somewhat clumsy vehicle, patented by a professional architect named Joseph Hansom in 1834. It was designed as a safety vehicle, having such large wheels that it was almost impossible to overturn. In a later version the whole structure was much lighter and the driving seat placed at the rear of the passenger compartment, thus allowing a clear view ahead and a certain amount of privacy. Although mainly used as a public conveyance, seating either one or two passengers, a large number were also privately owned and coach-man-driven. Some enthusiasts of the 1890s were wealthy amateurs

Fig. 22. Hansom cab.

49

who drove them as a hobby, in much the same way as titled noblemen drove stage-coaches during the 1800s.

The passenger compartment of the average hansom was entered through flap doors at the front. A later version was entered through an ordinary carriage door on the left-hand or near side of the vehicle. This was sometimes known as a **brougham-hansom** or **bow-fronted hansom** (plate 10), the curved front being enclosed and bow-shaped. The latter was considered even safer and more comfortable than the standard version.

The Gurney cab

Closely related to the Hansom cab, the Gurney cab had a pair of large wheels and was normally driven to a single horse. The driver's seat, however, was at the front while the passenger compartment was entered by means of a rear door and step. Similar to the American cab but with larger wheels and a lower, more comfortable driving seat, it was introduced during the 1880s but did not seriously challenge the hansom.

Fig. 23. Gurney cab.

The sedan cab

Another challenger to the hansom, about the same period as the Gurney cab, the sedan cab had the driving seat at the front and was entered through a rear door, passengers faced forward. Seats were in two hinged sections, lowered only after passengers entered the interior. It seated two inside.

The three-wheeled hansom

This was an ungainly version of the Hansom cab, running on three wheels, and was popular for a short period during the 1900s (plate 11). It was designed to seat four passengers, with a luggage rack on the roof. The box or driving seat was at the front of the passenger compartment, directly above the front wheel. The rear axle was cranked with suspension in the form of two full elliptical springs. The forecarriage had a form of suspension based on coil springs. An important feature was the low door and step at the front for easy access. The door was fitted at an angle of about forty-five degrees to the rest of the passenger compartment. A notable example is preserved in the Hull Transport Museum, registered as late as 1916.

The four-wheeled cab or 'growler'

Usually known as a 'four-wheeler', this cab replaced the hackney cab and was similar to the privately owned clarence. Used in the larger towns and cities from the 1840s until the appearance of motor cabs or taxis during the 1900s, some lingered until the 1920s and early 1930s. Later models were fitted with taxi-meters similar to those of motor vehicles.

During the second half of the nineteenth century growlers were often dirty and disreputable. Standards varied but many drivers not only kept untidy cabs, the floors littered with dirty straw, but were given to coarse language and abusing those unable or unwilling to offer large tips.

Although a number of cabs were in private ownership the majority were either hired out to their drivers or driven by employees. The average cab horse was often an animal that had seen better days in a gentleman's stable, frequently overloaded and overworked. The drivers working for large establishments were often brutal or careless and saw nothing of their horses out of

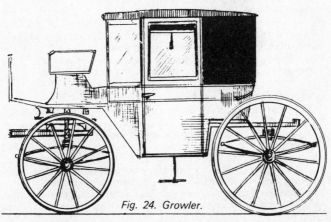

Fig. 24. Growler.

working hours, as they were looked after in stables by a staff of grooms and strappers. When the driver appeared in the morning his horse and cab would be ready for the road, harnessed to the last buckle. Horses driven in hansoms were usually of much better quality than ordinary cab horses and also younger.

The omnibus

George Shillibeer, an ex-naval man turned coach-builder, introduced omnibuses from Paris to London. His intention was to provide an alternative to the hackney cab and short stage-coach, which might prove more comfortable and less expensive. He went into business with two four-wheeled single-deckers which ran between Paddington and the Bank of England (plate 12). Services commenced on 4th July 1829, along a route already covered by a short stage-coach and later by the patent steam-carriage of Walter Hancock.

Each coach was drawn by bay horses, harnessed three abreast in French style. There was accommodation for twenty-two passengers, all seated inside on cushions and paying at least a third less than outside passengers on the short stage-coach. Drivers and conductors, unlike the hackney coachmen, were sober, clean and dressed in smart uniforms. The latest newspapers were always available to passengers, free of charge. Despite badly fitting windows, the 'Shillibeers' were an immediate success, soon making over a hundred pounds per week for twelve each-way journeys per day. Unfortunately three-horse buses were held to be dangerous and later banned from the streets by the newly formed Metropolitan Police. They were, however, revived towards the end of the century, but only in small numbers.

Shillibeer, nothing daunted, then introduced a batch of two-horse vehicles that would take up to sixteen passengers. These buses, unlike their predecessors, were perchless, having elliptical springs at the front and semi-elliptical springs at the back, attached directly to the axles. Seating was still longitudinal, as in the first 'Shillibeers', with a rear entrance and step. Two extra passengers were often carried at the front next to the driver.

Later omnibuses

The next development in public transport was the so-called **knifeboard omnibus,** also of French design adapted to English conditions. This was a double-decker of the 1850s, with low back-to-back seating on the roof, reached by a vertical ladder. It needed great agility to reach the upper deck, which was out of the question for most older men or for women with hampering skirts and false modesty. Speed of travel was about eight miles per hour. The front or forecarriage of the knifeboard had two elliptical springs and a transverse cross-spring. There were seats for two on the box, including the driver.

A great improvement on the knifeboard omnibus was the **garden-seat bus,** having double rows of forward facing seats on the upper deck (plate 13). This remained popular until motor-buses took over in the period shortly before the First World War. Garden-seat buses had safe outside steps, guarded by a handrail, and a decency board, which prevented women from making an unnecessary display of ankles and petticoats. The driver sat very high on a single box-seat, directly in front of the upper-deck passengers. Most vehicles were plastered with advertisements for branded goods, having a distinctly commercial appearance. By the 1880s the step at the back for the conductor had given way to the more familiar rear platform. Garden-seat buses ran from 1881 until 1914 although discarded by the London General Omnibus Company in 1911.

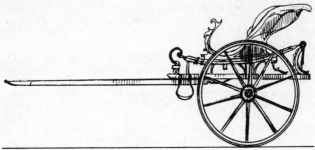

Fig. 25. Continental chaise

7. Privately driven carriages

Some of the finest and most typical vehicles of this type began to appear during the second half of the eighteenth century. This was the beginning of an era when driving ceased to be a mere chore, and became an increasing pastime and pleasure. Naturally enough it was a period of improved road-making.

From the 1780s privately owned and driven four-wheeled vehicles were known as 'phaetons'. In Greek legend Phaeton was the son of Helios, coachman to the sun god and driver of the sun chariot. An impetuous youth, he begged permission to drive the sun but lost control of his team and nearly set the world on fire in the ensuing crash. Drivers of such carriages were thought to have a devil-may-care attitude, resembling that of Phaeton, after whom their vehicle was named.

Some of these vehicles were driven by professional coachmen, including the four-wheeled dogcart and various brakes. These, however, would be informal occasions and coachmen-in-charge would not wear full livery. Four-wheeled dogcarts often served as station wagons or for light passenger work on a large estate.

The continental chaise

Introduced between 1760 and 1780 the continental chaise (plate 14) descended from the Italian *carretta*, drawn by a pony or mule. A comparatively light vehicle for its day, it was popular in both England and France until the period of the French Revolution. The often single seat and low dashboard were suspended above a wooden underframe by means of strong leather braces. The English version was solid and perhaps safer, but had higher sides with wheels much further to the rear. This made the centre of

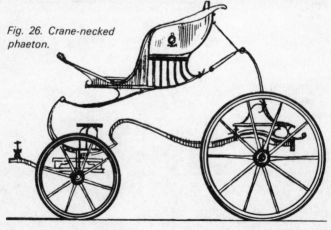

Fig. 26. Crane-necked phaeton.

gravity too low and strained the back of the single horse. Some later versions were hooded. A footstep on the near side was little more than a metal ring set at an angle of forty-five degrees to the underframe. Shafts tended to be straight rather than curved, especially on earlier models. The framework was often ornate with carved wood and painted surfaces.

The crane-necked phaeton

This was an essentially sporting vehicle of the 1780s and 1790s, used for the sake of driving with a turn of speed. It was four-wheeled with a high seat for two, suspended well above ground level. While an earlier version was built with a heavy perch or undercarriage, the popular type had curved irons or cranes under which the forewheels could turn in full lock — a dangerous and unstable design. Front wheels were up to five feet in diameter while rear wheels were sometimes as much as eight feet high, although usually about six feet. Both types were known as 'high flyers', a nickname also given to the daring young men and occasionally young women who drove them. Perhaps the best known female driver of the period was the notorious Lady Archer, 'as renowned for her skill with the whip as for the cosmetic powers she exercised upon her complexion.'

The crane-necked phaeton was a popular mode of transport with the Prince of Wales (later Prince Regent and George IV) and his circle. Phaetons could be driven to either a pair or four-in-hand. Some attempted to drive them to a team of six but the leading pair was usually in the charge of a postilion.

Fig. 27. High cocking cart.

The high cocking cart

A two-wheeled vehicle for driver and single passenger, the high cocking cart resembled the detached front half of a stage-coach or brake. It came into vogue during the early 1790s, slightly later than the 'high flyer'. The high seat was raised above a boot with slatted sides, in which fighting cocks were carried to a match or main. It was driven to a single horse or tandem, often at breakneck speeds. A version of the cocking cart, native to Ireland, was the **suicide gig,** which had an even higher driving seat with a rear seat for the groom.

The curricle

The curricle (plate 15), both as a two-wheeled carriage and mode of draught gear, was thought to have been invented in Italy during the second half of the eighteenth century. It became popular in England during the 1800s, especially after its patronage by the Prince Regent. It was hooded, comparatively low-slung and had a rear seat for a diminutive groom or 'tiger'. A reaction to high gigs and cocking carts, the curricle had a reputation for being smart and fast, yet easy to control. It remained popular for about forty years and was driven to a pair of horses.

The cabriolet

The cabriolet (plate 16) appeared during the second decade of the nineteenth century and at one time threatened to oust the curricle. Like the curricle it was nearly always hooded, and also a two-wheeler, driven to a single horse. Its first notable sponsor was Count d'Orsay, a French nobleman who settled in London, where he became a leader of taste and fashion. Count d'Orsay delighted to drive large and powerful horses, in the care of almost dwarfish 'tigers'. Frequently driven at night by gay bachelors, an important feature was a warning bell attached to the horse collar. Similar bells were later carried by Hansom cabs, especially those with rubber tyres.

Fig. 28. Cabriolet.

Fig. 29. Caned whiskey.

The whiskey

The whiskey was a light gig similar in outward form to the earlier curricle but drawn by a single horse or pony. The body was fixed directly to the shafts and decorated with a pattern of woven canework, otherwise known as a **caned whiskey.** Used for short journeys at high speed its name derived from the way in which it whisked over the ground. It became popular from about 1812. A slightly earlier **grasshopper whiskey** was even lighter but had plain sides.

The Dennet gig

The early type of gig was mainly a sporting affair. Later, however, the name was bestowed on any light or cheap two-wheeled carriage, often driven by those who could afford nothing better. If such a vehicle cost less than £12 to build it was taxed very low at only a few shillings per annum, but had to be painted with the slogan 'tax cart'. Gigs from the second decade of the

Fig. 30. Plain gig (1820).

nineteenth century were much better designed and nearer the standards of a gentleman's carriage. Dennet gigs, introduced about 1814, were of this improved type and could be driven in town or country, usually to a single horse. Although designed by a coach-builder named Bennett, they are thought to have been named after three fashionable sisters, also actresses, known as Dennet.

The Stanhope gig

Introduced about 1816 this two-wheeled gig (plate 18) was constructed by a coach-builder named Tilbury to the designs of the Hon. Fitzroy Stanhope. It was hung on four springs, often had a serviceable hood and was much heavier than the Dennet gig. The driving seat was designed as a rib-backed chair.

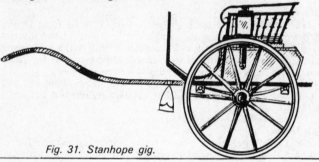

Fig. 31. Stanhope gig.

The tilbury

This was also made by Tilbury of London, responsible for the stanhope and other light carriages of the period. It was one of the most popular vehicles of its type in Europe, especially in Spain, Italy and Portugal, as it could be driven in comfort over the roughest roads. Introduced about 1820, it was mounted on six undersprings and had an ample rib-backed seat, but neither hood nor boot. After the cabriolet it was the heaviest two-wheeled vehicle of the period, mainly on account of the ironwork for its suspension.

The Lawton gig and the Liverpool gig

These were both very much the same type of vehicle, introduced about 1860. Lawton was the designer and builder of the type named after him, and he started coachbuilding in Liverpool, hence the name Liverpool gig. Lawton vehicles are recognised as the Rolls-Royces of English horse-drawn vehicles.

Fig. 32. Liverpool gig.

The buggy

The buggy was a two-wheeled low sprung hooded vehicle and was mainly used towards the end of the nineteenth century. The so-called **Duke of York's buggy,** made by Lawton and Goodman of London, was a fairly high gig but without a hood. It was a sporting vehicle favoured by Lord Lonsdale in his epic race against time — for a wager — in 1891. The **Connaught buggy** was a more conventional hooded vehicle, designed for H.R.H. the Duchess of Connaught, which she drove mainly in India. The American buggy is mentioned in a later chapter.

The sulky

This has been used from 1800 to the present day, although modern versions have greatly changed in appearance. Extremely light, it was a two-wheeled vehicle driven by a single person, without room for either groom or passenger. It was widely used for training purposes, harness racing and time trials. The original sulky was slung high on large wheels, while the modern version is much smaller with wire-spoked wheels.

The pony phaeton

Phaetons, first popular during the 1780s, went out of fashion during the second decade of the nineteenth century, to be revived — often in smaller versions — ten or twelve years later. One of the first of these later types was a pony phaeton driven by George IV. Although as Prince Regent George IV preferred a curricle, towards the end of his reign he became too stout to drive a more sporting vehicle. The great advantage of the pony phaeton both to the stout and elderly, and also to ladies with flowing skirts, was its low-slung bodywork, having a footstep merely a few inches above the ground. Wheels were protected by large splashers or mudguards. They were twenty-two inches in diameter at the front and thirty-three inches in diameter at the back. Such vehicles usually had a large hood, high dashboard and protective leather apron.

A small basketwork pony phaeton was eventually introduced, designed for driving children either on an estate or down country lanes. It was easy to enter for even the smallest child and had few exposed areas of paintwork to smear and scratch.

The mail phaeton

This was a massive vehicle of the late 1820s, built on the lines of a coach, with either a perch or solid undercarriage. It was a vehicle for a strong and experienced male driver, used for exercising coach-horses or for carrying local mail in a large underboot. It was usually driven to a pair of horses harnessed to a coach pole with chains rather than leather traces. It had a high seat in the front and a low seat behind, with accommodation for three passengers and a driver. The **Beaufort mail phaeton,** designed for the Duke of Beaufort later in the nineteenth century, was even larger than the standard model with room for two extra people.

The demi-mail phaeton

This was slightly smaller than the mail phaeton, fitted with elliptical springs at front and back. It seated three or four people, having a front seat in the form of a rib-backed chair. Considered more elegant than the mail phaeton and Beaufort mail phaeton, it was driven almost exclusively in towns, often by ladies, and was introduced about 1832.

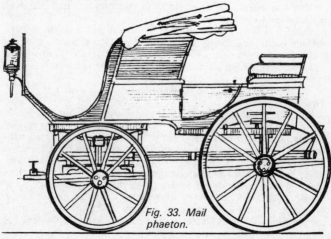

Fig. 33. Mail phaeton.

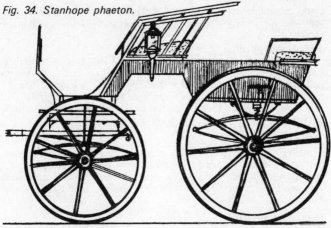

Fig. 34. Stanhope phaeton.

The Stanhope phaeton

Another popular vehicle by Tilbury, this was designed for the **Honourable Fitzroy Stanhope, about 1830. It was even lighter** than the demi-mail phaeton, frequently driven to a single horse. It had elliptical springs under the front and rear parts, normally seating a driver, passenger and two attendants. Seating was of a rounded, rib-backed type at the front, while rear seating had a single rail. It was provided either with or without a hood. Shafts

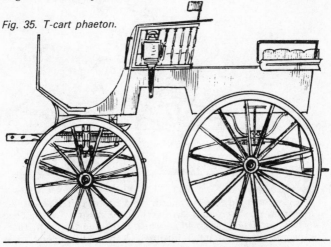

Fig. 35. T-cart phaeton.

could be attached to open-ended futchells, on the forecarriage —
removed for handy storage. It was essentially a town and park
vehicle.

The T-cart phaeton

Designed by a guards officer about 1880, this was mainly
fashionable in military circles. It was similar to the Stanhope
phaeton, being constructed for a single horse, not more than 14
hands high (one hand equals 4 inches). The seat at the front had
room for two, while the seat at the back was single, hence the T
shape.

The park phaeton

A larger version of the pony phaeton, introduced about 1833,
the park phaeton was driven almost exclusively by ladies to a pair
of matching ponies. This was a summer vehicle and rarely seen
with hood or apron. There was no rear seat and a mounted groom
followed on horseback.

The spider phaeton

An elegant four-wheeled vehicle of the 1880s, the spider
phaeton was a tilbury body with a groom's seat at the rear,
mounted on arched irons. It was often used for showing the paces
of a fast well-bred horse, and was much favoured by Lord
Lonsdale during the 1890s.

*Fig. 36. Spider
phaeton.*

Cars and carts

These were mainly used as country and estate vehicles, built in a
wide variety of shapes and sizes. While the majority of gigs had
only two occupants, carts and cars held three, four and sometimes
five people. They were much favoured by the farming community

although sporting farmers frequently drove such gigs as the stanhope and tilbury.

The dogcart

Introduced during the 1800s, this was first used for carrying gun-dogs on a shooting expedition, having a large underboot with slatted side vents (plate 22). There were both two-wheeled and four-wheeled varieties, the former driven to a single horse while the latter could be driven to a pair. The four-wheeled type seated either four or six, including the driver. The smaller, more popular version had a double driving seat and two seats facing backwards, having a raised footboard and common back-rest. The six-seater dogcart, of which only a few were made, was a larger but lower vehicle with a double driving seat and back-to-back seating at the rear. All types had elliptical springs at both back and front.

Fig. 37. Dogcart.
Fig. 38. Four-wheeled dogcart (rear spokes removed to show suspension).

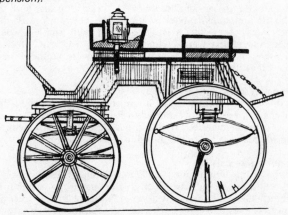

Fig. 39. Manchester market cart.

The Manchester market cart

A panel-sided vehicle of the 1870s, suitable for trade and business purposes, and much favoured by country shopkeepers, it was in effect, a cheaper variety of dogcart, selling for about £12. It seated four people, including the driver, with two facing backwards. Normally there was a low rail in place of a dashboard, and the cart was driven to a single pony.

The ralli car or cart

Usually known as a 'car', although there has been much controversy on this subject, this was introduced about 1898 (plate 23). It was similar to the smaller or two-wheeled dogcart, with rear footboard and back-to-back seating. The bodywork was slung slightly lower than the average dogcart, with smaller wheels. Curved side panels were inclined outwards over the wheels on either side. The gracefully curving shafts were attached inside rather than outside or under the bodywork.

The royalty cart

Similar to the ralli car, but with much larger wheels and a high dashboard, it was widely exported to Europe and North America, and was much favoured by the Prince de Rohan of Bohemia, a noted whip of his day. It was introduced about 1890.

The governess cart

This was introduced about 1900 and specially designed for the use of children, frequently driven by the nursery governess (plate 25). Fairly low and entered by a rear door, it was mainly confined to country lanes and parks, where it was considered the safest of

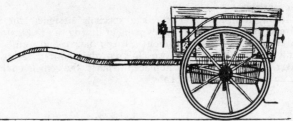

Fig. 40. Governess cart.

all owner-driven carriages. Usually drawn by a stocky pony noted for its quietness and good manners, it was sometimes known as a tub car or cart. Passengers and driver shared longitudinal side seats, facing inwards.

The Eridge cart

A type of pony phaeton of the 1890s invented by Lord Abergavenny, its main undercarriage was similar to that of the standard phaeton, but it also had back-to-back seating in the style of a dogcart. Elliptical springs supported both front and rear parts of the vehicle. Other features of importance were the low step, a hand-lever brake operating on the back wheels and splashers over the wheels at back and front. It was driven to a single pony.

The village phaeton

A four-wheeled vehicle of the 1890s, this was built to carry six passengers, two of whom faced the driver. An underboot was useful for small items of hand luggage. It was suitable for lady drivers, as it was fairly low and easy to enter, and was driven to a single horse.

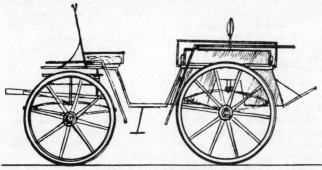

Fig. 41. Village phaeton.

The parisian

An elegant, low-slung carriage specially designed for lady drivers, the parisian was mainly popular during the 1880s. It was driven to a single pony of about thirteen hands, and would normally seat two adults and two children, the children facing the driver. If a pole were used in place of shafts, the vehicle could be driven to a pair of light cobs.

Fig. 42. Float.

The float

The float was introduced about 1890 as a utilitarian two-wheeled vehicle, used by farmers for marketing and by dairymen with milk rounds (plate 24). Like the governess cart it was low at the back and entered through a rear door, but unlike the governess cart, seats faced forward for both passengers and driver. In towns they were usually driven from a standing position, allowing the driver a better view of traffic ahead. Although originally country vehicles, a number were still used on city milk rounds until the 1950s. Some later versions had cranked axles. Most had splashers or mudguards. They were driven to a single horse or pony.

The wagonette

The first vehicle of this type was introduced about 1842, designed by the firm of Amershams for Lord Curzon. In 1845 Messrs Hoopers of London built a similar vehicle to the orders of Queen Victoria and the specifications of the Prince Consort. The original version was used either for several passengers and a quantity of hand luggage, or larger items of luggage only. This made it useful both as a station wagon and luggage cart, and also for picnics and sight-seeing expeditions. Seats on both sides were longitudinal and inward-facing, with a raised box-seat for the driver. On some versions the seats could be taken out. It was driven either to a pair or a single horse. A later version, which was known as the **Lonsdale wagonette,** could be driven unicorn or to a four-in-hand.

The brougham wagonette

A closed version of the wagonette, introduced about 1877, this was often constructed with a circular or bow-shaped front, also as a convertible for open use in fine weather. It normally seated six persons inside, with room for two more on the driving seat. Priced about ninety guineas it was one of the cheapest four-wheeled carriages on the market. A contemporary brougham, seating only two, would cost in the region of a hundred and forty guineas.

The char-a-banc

Introduced during the 1840s, this French version of the wagonette was mainly used for country driving, and was popular for attending shooting parties and other sporting events. It was usually driven to a four-in-hand, and had cross seats for seven, including the driver, with a groom's seat at the rear. Sometimes it had a slatted under-compartment for sporting dogs, as with the four-wheeled dogcart.

While the char-a-banc was at first used exclusively by large and wealthy establishments, it was later fitted with extra seating for school parties and works outings. One of the first vehicles of this type was presented to Queen Victoria by King Louis Philippe of France. A similar vehicle was the roof seat brake.

Fig. 43. Roof seat brake.

Fig. 44. Body brake.

Brakes (or 'breaks')

These were somewhat ungainly versions of the first wagonette, introduced during the late 1860s. They were general utility vehicles and driven either by the owner or a professional coachman. They were used for exercising coach or carriage horses, either as a pair or four-in-hand, and sometimes for taking staff and extra luggage or furniture from house to house. This would be in the days when a person of wealth and standing would have a town house, a country house and hunting or shooting lodge.

The **skeleton brake** was used for training horses, mainly by professional horse-dealers and breakers. This was little more than a framework with a high box-seat at the front and small rear platform. It was driven to a pair of horses harnessed to pole gear, one of which would be an older, more experienced animal — serving as much as the driver to train its younger partner. A groom stood on the platform ready to jump down and run to the horses' heads in case of trouble. The author recollects seeing one of these in daily use in Leamington Spa during the 1940s.

The **body brake** was a larger version of the standard brake, with longitudinal seats, facing inwards. It was mainly used for sight-seeing trips, public outings and even for military purposes. It was entered, like a wagonette, by means of a rear door and steps. A type known as the shooting brake had an underboot and slatted sides. Both the above could be driven to either a pair or four-in-hand.

The private drag or park drag

A small, neat version of the stage-coach (plate 27), introduced after the decline of public coaching, during the 1860s, it was widely used for private driving marathons and other sporting purposes, also as a grandstand at race meetings and cricket matches. The luggage boot under the rear seats could be used for picnic hampers, while the locker lid served as a folding table. It was usually painted in subdued colours, sometimes in the livery of a titled family, and was driven as a four-in-hand.

In former days many units of the British Army owned a private coach or drag, known as the **regimental coach,** used by officers for pleasure driving or as a grandstand. Survivors into the second half of the twentieth century were run by the Royal Horse Guards (now the Blues and Royals), the Royal Artillery, and the Royal Army Service Corps (now the Royal Corps of Transportation). Coaching marathons are still a feature of certain agricultural and horse shows such as the Royal Show and the Royal Windsor Horse Show.

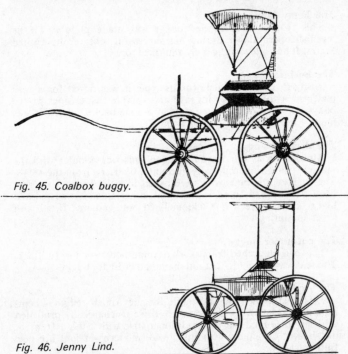

Fig. 45. Coalbox buggy.

Fig. 46. Jenny Lind.

8. American carriages

American vehicles are included in a separate category to avoid confusion. Not only do they have strong national characteristics but they are also dissimilar from other types in many points of construction, use and design. Traditional European types of owner-driven and coachman-driven carriage would only appear in more conservative centres of the former colonial states.

The coalbox buggy
A lightweight, showy four-wheeled vehicle, this derived its name from its resemblance to a grocer's coalbox, of a type seen in village stores during the nineteenth century. It was frequently painted red or blue with gold stripes or lining.

The Jenny Lind
This type of four-wheeled buggy was made popular by the Swedish opera singer during her successful tour of the United States. It had a low-slung body and fixed top.

The business buggy
A smart, elegant vehicle for its type, it was noted for a rear platform with space for luggage and sample cases. Sides of the bodywork were caned in the style of a cane-backed chair. It was made with an ample folding hood.

The doctor's buggy
Also known as the 'doctor's wagon' this was popular with the medical profession, especially in country districts, from the 1890s. The sides of the bodywork were caned to waist level. An ample hood usually had small windows on either side. It was painted black or dark green but seldom lined out, and was fitted with silver mountings.

The cut-under buggy
This had an arched framework or underbody to allow full lock. The seat was much higher than that of an ordinary buggy.

The Amish buggy
This is still used by and made for the Amish religious community, forbidden by their creed to drive mechanically propelled vehicles. It is made in the traditional style with a high front or dashboard. Originally without a hood, modern versions are now fully enclosed.

The jump-seat wagon

A light, near equirotal wagon with a fixed top, this could be converted into a single-seater by sliding the front and back seats together.

The surrey

The best-known version, made famous by the song, was the **fringe-top,** the fixed roof being ornamented with deep side fringes. A four-seater family vehicle, it had a high leather dashboard and sweeping splashers or fenders (mudguards) to protect the passengers from mud and dust. It was often furnished with fitted rugs and elaborate brass oil lamps. A cheaper version, without a top, was known as the **spring wagon** or 'poor man's surrey'. The pony surrey was a smaller type drawn by either one or two ponies.

Fig. 47.
Fringe-top
surrey.

The buckboard

A low-slung but strongly made vehicle used for country road work, it had strong front bracing, which reduced vibration and noise. There were several versions but most were near equirotal.

The jogging cart

A light two-wheeled vehicle used for exercising trotting horses, it had its single or double seat very near the axle and slightly lower than the wheel tops.

The bike wagon

A near equirotal wagon of the 1890s, seating either one or two, the bike wagon's main features were curved or cranked 'bike' axles and pneumatic tyres.

The rockaway

Also known as the **depot wagon,** this was a four-wheeled, four-seater vehicle used for taking passengers and their luggage to the nearest railroad station or depot. The roof was a hard, fixed top. A larger version was the three-seat **platform wagon,** which was nearly ten feet long. A four-seat platform wagon was used in certain areas, especially holiday resorts, as a hired wagon for sightseeing. An American version of the English wagonette was the side-seated platform wagon.

The concord

This was the North American version of the stage-coach, adapted to colonial conditions. Named after its place of origin, the New Hampshire town of Concord, it was designed for nine inside passengers, drawn by a team of six horses. The almost egg-shaped body with strongly curved sides, was suspended on two sets of longitudinal leather straps or thoroughbraces, attached to inflexible metal standards. A larger version was used in the far West, and also exported to South Africa. A light concord was used in country districts of the eastern states, being smaller than the standard version and sometimes drawn by four horses. An open-sided public coach, otherwise similar to the concord, was known as the **mud wagon.** Some of the finest vehicles of this type were constructed by the firm of Abbot-Downing.

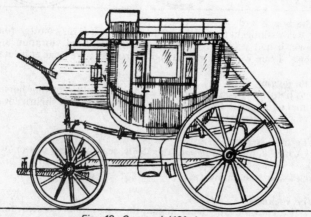

Fig. 48. Concord (13ft long).

9. Where to see coaches and carriages

Coaches and carriages from the **Royal Mews at Buckingham Palace** are to be seen on many state occasions throughout the year and at special events such as the State Opening of Parliament, royal weddings, jubilees and the official visits made by crowned heads and other distinguished visitors. Newly appointed ambassadors to the Court of St James are always taken to present their credentials in a coach or carriage, usually a state landau with liveried coachman and footmen in attendance. Rehearsals for these events need periods of exercise and training, both in London streets and parks, often undertaken with lighter vehicles such as a brake or wagonette. A clarence in daily use conveys official dispatch boxes between Buckingham Palace and various ministries. Both the carriage-house and the stables of the Royal Mews are open to the public on Wednesday and Thursday afternoons throughout the year from 2 p.m. to 4 p.m. except during Royal Ascot Week.

Carriages in action

Agricultural and horse shows throughout the country frequently have displays and competitions for harness classes, sometimes with a marathon drive for private coaches and four-in-hand teams, which end with awarding prizes and a parade in the main show ring. National and local driving clubs sometimes stage rallies and meets, usually in connection with larger shows but often independently. Driving round obstacle courses with the lighter, owner-driven type of carriage is now a popular feature of the Horse of the Year Show and other similar shows, both indoor and outdoor.

Museums with carriage collections

Arlington Court, Arlington, near Barnstaple, Devon EX31 4LP. Telephone: Shirwell (027 182) 296. A National Trust house with a representative cross-section of many horse-drawn vehicles, especially from the nineteenth century, displayed in a coach house and loft. The stables are on show and carriage rides given on estate roads.

Bath Carriage Museum, Circus Mews, Bath, Avon. Telephone: Bath (0225) 25175. Housed in the Mews built by Wood the Younger in 1759, this is one of the most comprehensive collections of horse-drawn vehicles in Britain, together with harness, whips, lamps and liveries. Items include a clarence, victoria, hansom cab, black Maria and the Duke of Somerset's state coach. Many of the carriages are used for filming, promotions and television. Carriage rides available and stables open throughout the season.

Birmingham Museum of Science and Industry, Newhall Street, Birmingham B3 1RZ. Telephone: 021-236 1022. A four-wheeled dogcart.

Breamore House, Breamore, near Fordingbridge, Hampshire. Telephone: Downton (0725) 22270. Housed in extensive stables dating back to the seventeenth century. Most vehicles are of nineteenth century origins. Outstanding exhibits include 'The Red Rover' London to Southampton coach.

Bristol Industrial Museum, Prince's Wharf, Bristol, Avon BS1 4RN. Telephone: Bristol (0272) 299771, extension 290. Among the collection of horse-drawn vehicles is the pioneer caravan 'The Wanderer'.

Buckland Abbey, Yelverton, Devon PL20 6EY. Telephone: Yelverton (082 285) 3607. Selection of carriages and other horse-drawn vehicles.

Croxteth Hall and Country Park, Croxteth, Liverpool L12 0HB. Telephone: 051-228 5311. Several carriages formerly used by the Sefton family and others from the County Museum's collection.

Flambards Victorian Village, Aero Park, Culdrose Manor, Helston, Cornwall TR13 0GA. Telephone: Helston (032 65) 4549. Several carriages in reconstructed, c1900 village.

Gawsworth Hall, near Macclesfield, Cheshire. Telephone: North Rode (026 03) 456. A collection of coaches and unique fleet of Victorian garden seat omnibuses.

Glasgow Museum of Transport, 25 Albert Drive, Glasgow G41 2PE. Telephone: 041-423 8000. Large collection of horse-drawn pleasure carriages and commercial vehicles, including family coaches and a private omnibus.

Gunnersbury Park Museum, Gunnersbury Park, London W3 8LQ. Telephone: 01-992 1612. A posting chariot and a town chariot used by the Rothschild family, a hansom cab by Forder, a pony phaeton (all restored), and a Bath chair.

Hereford and Worcester County Museum, Hartlebury Castle, Hartlebury, near Kidderminster, Worcestershire DY11 7XZ. Telephone: Hartlebury (0299) 250416. Large selection of horse-drawn vehicles of all periods, including a station bus, hansom cab, horse-drawn ambulance and travelling chariot.

Hull Transport and Archaeology Museum, 36 High Street, Hull, North Humberside HU1 1NQ. Telephone: Hull (0482) 223111, extension 2737. Wide range of carriages including a stage coach, a carretta, dress chariot and a rare three-wheeled hansom cab.

Ipswich Museum, High Street, Ipswich, Suffolk IP1 3QH. Telephone: Ipswich (0473) 213761. A selection of interesting horse-drawn carriages.

Killiow Country Park, Kea, near Truro, Cornwall TR3 6AG. Telephone: The Ben Ford collection of coaches, carriages and other horse-drawn vehicles, used in films and television productions. Carriage rides.

Leicestershire Museum of Technology, Abbey Pumping Station, Corporation Road, Abbey Lane, Leicester. Telephone: Leicester (0533) 61330. A selection of carriages including a hansom cab, clarence and dress chariot.

London Transport Museum, Covent Garden, London WC2E 7BB. Telephone: 01-379 6344. Horse-drawn omnibuses of various types and scale models.

Manx Museum (and its branches), Douglas, Isle of Man. Telephone: Douglas (0624) 75522. Horse-drawn vehicles formerly used in the island.

Museum of East Anglian Life, Stowmarket, Suffolk IP14 1DL. Telephone: Stowmarket (0449) 612229. Horse-drawn vehicles associated with East Anglia.

Museum of London, London Wall, London EC2Y 5HN. Telephone: 01-600 3699. The Lord Mayor's coach.

North of England Open Air Museum, Beamish, near Stanley, County Durham. Telephone: Stanley (0207) 31811. Several horse-drawn vehicles. Carriage rides during the summer.

Preston Hall Museum, Preston Park, Yarm Road, Stockton-on-Tees, Cleveland. Telephone: Stockton-on-Tees (0642) 781184. Selection of private carriages and other horse-drawn vehicles.

Raby Castle, Staindrop, near Darlington, County Durham. Telephone: Staindrop (0833) 60202. Interesting collection of horse-drawn vehicles, mainly private carriages, including a travelling coach, a state coach and a good collection of tack.

Royal Mews, Buckingham Palace Road, London SW1. Telephone: 01-930 4832, extension 634. State carriages and harness and horse-drawn vehicles in daily use including broughams, brakes and clarences.

Salford Museum and Art Gallery, Peel Park, The Crescent, Salford M5 4WU. Telephone: 061-736 2649. Carriages feature in a reconstructed period street.

Science Museum, Exhibition Road, South Kensington, London SW7 2DD. Telephone: 01-589 3456. One of the largest collections in the country but only a few vehicles are on show at any one time because of shortage of space. There are numerous scale models to explain the development of coaches and carriages.

Shire Horse Farm and Carriage Museum, Lower Grillis Farm, Treskilland, Redruth, Cornwall. Telephone: Camborne (0209) 713606. Various horse-drawn vehicles including several private carriages.

Spye Park Stables Museum, Chittoe, near Chippenham, Wiltshire. Telephone: Lacock (024 973) 247. A collection mainly of private carriages.

Staffordshire County Museum, Shugborough, Stafford. Telephone: Little Haywood (0889) 881388. A collection of carriages, including a dress chariot.

Tolson Memorial Museum, Ravensknowle Park, Huddersfield, West Yorkshire HD5 8DJ. Telephone: Huddersfield (0484) 30591. Interesting examples of horse-drawn vehicles.

Tyrwhitt-Drake Museum of Carriages, Archbishop's Stables, Mill Street, Maidstone, Kent. Telephone: Maidstone (0622) 54497. A comprehensive collection of coaches and carriages, including state coaches and dress chariots.

Ulster Folk and Transport Museum, Cultra Manor, Holywood, County Down BT18 0EU. Telephone: Holywood (023 17) 5411. Also at Witham Street, Belfast BT4 1HP. Telephone: Belfast (0232) 51519. Horse-drawn vehicles associated with the life of Northern Ireland.

York Castle Museum, Tower Street, York. Telephone: York (0904) 53611. Horse-drawn carriages in reconstructed Victorian and Edwardian streets.

Yorkshire Museum of Carriages and Horse-drawn Vehicles, Yore Mill, Aysgarth Fall, Aysgarth, Leyburn, North Yorkshire. Telephone: Richmond (0748) 3275. A comprehensive collection of over 45 vehicles, coachman and owner driven, trade and private. With examples from five countries, together with harness and liveries.

Glossary

Arm: spindle upon which a wheel turns.

Axle-box: box into which the end of an axle is fitted.

Axle-pivot: centre on which forewheels turn. Part of the forecarriage.

Axle-tree: there are two main forms, one in which the spindle is supported by a wooden beam, and the other in which the wheels are attached to either end of a beam.

Box: raised seat from which a coach or carriage is driven.

Chamfer: the shaving or carving of wheel spokes to lighten their weight and improve appearance.

Chassis: the underframe of a vehicle.

Colletts: metal bands used for securing the hub of a wheel.

Cranes: iron underframes of a carriage curved or raised to allow underlock of the forewheels.

Dashboard: raised front to the footboard of a driving seat.

Dish: inward or concave slope of wheel-spokes.

Equirotal carriage: four-wheeled vehicle with both front and back wheels of equal size (forewheels are usually smaller than rear wheels); mainly associated with coaches of the sixteenth century but later revived, by W. Bridges Adams — although never popular — during the mid nineteenth century. The Duke of Wellington owned an equirotal carriage in 1838. Several American buggies were equirotal.

Fellowes: sections of a wheel rim into which spokes are fitted.

Footboard: a raised board at the front of a driving seat, or rear seat of a dogcart, to support the feet of a driver or passenger.

Futchell or **Futchel:** prong-like parts of the forecarriage to which draught gear may be attached.

Guard: official of a mail-coach or stage-coach who is responsible for the mails, luggage and well-being of passengers.

Headed: covered with a roof.

Leaf springs: springs made from flat, curved plates of tempered steel; either elliptical or semi-elliptical.

Lock: the angle through which the forewheels of a vehicle may be turned.

Mews: formerly a place where hawks were kept (mewed) but later a combined coach-house and stables.

Nave: the centre of a wheel (either wood or metal).

Park coach: also a park drag. A private coach driven to a four-in-hand; kept for mainly sporting purposes.

Perch: also an underperch. Bar or framework supporting the underbody of a coach or carriage.

Pole: centre bar to which a pair of horses may be harnessed, one on each side.

Post-horn: yard-long metal horn carried by the guard of a mail-coach or stage-coach, on which to sound warnings.

Rim: outer part of a wheel, next to the tyre.

Roller bolt: used in fastening traces of harness, thus connecting horse to vehicle.

Rumble: large outside seat at the back of a coach or carriage.

Skid-pan: metal shoe used in the form of a brake; fitted to the near-side back wheel on inclines; known in country districts as a 'drug-bat'.

Splinter bar: cross-beam of a forecarriage to which the shafts, pole or swingletrees may be fitted.

Swingletree: horizontal bar to which harness traces may be attached on certain types of vehicle, there being a bar to each horse.

Tiger: groom riding on the rear seat of a curricle or cabriolet; usually a short man or youth in charge of a tall, powerful horse.

Tooling: driving, i.e. tooling a tandem.

Tyre or **Tire:** metal band fixed to the outer rim of a wheel. Later tyres were made of solid rubber or were pneumatic, with inner tubes.

Wheel-plates: circular iron plates bolted under the forecarriage, on which the wheels of a vehicle turn.

Whipple-tree: an attachment for draught gear fixed to the forecarriage.

Bibliography

American Horse Drawn Vehicles; Jack D. Rittenhouse; Crown Publishers, New York, 1958.

An Assemblage of Nineteenth Century Horses and Carriages; Jennifer Lang (illustrations from the original sketches of William Francis Freelove); Perpetua Press, Farnham, 1971.

Army Service Corps Training — part III: *Transport;* HMSO, London, 1911.

A Book About Travelling, Past and Present; T. A. Croal; William P. Nimmo, London and Edinburgh, 1877.

Buses, Trolleys and Trams; Chas A. Dunbar; Weidenfeld and Nicolson, London, 1967.

Carriages; Jacques Damase; Weidenfeld and Nicolson, London, 1968.

Carriage Building in England and France; G. Hooper; London, 1890.

Carriages to the End of the Nineteenth Century; Philip Sumner BSc: HMSO (Science Museum Booklets), London, 1970.

Discovering Harness and Saddlery; Major G. Tylden; Shire Publications, Princes Risborough, 1971.

The Elegant Carriage; Marylian Watney; J. A. Allen, London, 1961.

English Pleasure Carriages; W. Bridges Adams; London, 1837 (reprinted by Adams and Dart, London, 1971, with introduction by Jack Simmons).

Guide to the Transport Museum, Hull; J. Bartlett MA, FSA, FMA; City of Hull Museums, Kingston-upon-Hull, 1971.

The History of Carriages; Laszlo Tarr, translated by Elisabeth Hoch; Vision Press, London, 1969, and Corvina Press, Budapest, 1969.

The History of Coaches; G. A. Thrupp; London, 1877.

The Horse Bus as a Vehicle; Charles Lee; British Transport Commission, London, 1962.

Horses of Britain (for notes on coach and carriage horses); Lady Wentworth; William Collins, London, 1944.

Horses and Saddlery; Major G. Tylden; J. A. Allen, London, 1965.

Modern Carriages; G. Hooper; London, 1888.

Notes on the Construction of Private Carriages in England; G. Hooper; London, 1876.

A Practical Treatise on Coach Building; J. W. Bruges; London, 1918.

Quicksilver, a Hundred Years of Coaching 1750-1850; R. C. and J. M. Anderson; David and Charles, Newton Abbot, 1973.

Roads and Vehicles; Anthony Bird; Longman Green, London and Harlow, 1969.

Thy Servant the Horse; Lionel Edwards; Country Life, London, 1952.

Transport; E. F. Hayward; Macmillan Educational Books, London and Basingstoke, 1972.

Index

INDEX

Printed by C. I. Thomas & Sons (Haverfordwest) Ltd.,
Press Buildings, Merlins Bridge, Haverfordwest, Dyfed.